100 POEMS TO GROW YOUR CONFIDENCE

100 POEMS TO GROW YOUR CONFIDENCE

EDITED BY LIZ ISON

BATSFORD

Introduction

Having self-confidence can make all the difference
to the way we live our lives. It really matters.
Confidence can make us feel good about ourselves,
encourage us to make a start, spur us on to follow our
dreams, enable us to take risks, or help us face up to
an uncertain future with courage and fortitude.

Some people can come across as more confident
than others, but it is also the case that confidence
levels fluctuate over time. Our levels of confidence
depend not only on our inner sense of self, but also
are influenced by whom we are with, what we are
doing and the challenges we are facing.

In these pages, you will find a range of poetic
explorations of confidence in all its guises. Our own
inner critic can often act as a brake on our self-
belief and courage so it is exciting to read poets who
feel and describe an easy sense of self-confidence.
Poems often feel like they are delivered direct to our
emotional bloodstreams, so who wouldn't feel a fillip
of confidence on reading Dylan Thomas's seductive
assertion, 'honoured among wagons I was prince
of the apple towns' ('Fern Hill'), or on listening to
Wordsworth telling us of his sense of joy, 'Bliss was
it in that dawn to be alive, / But to be young was
very heaven!' (*The Prelude*)? Poets draw energy and
confidence from the beauty and power of the world
around them, expressed by Edna St Vincent Millay

in her heady response to nature, 'Thou'st made the world too beautiful this year; / my soul is all but out of me' ('God's World').

In these examples confidence emanates from the joy of being alive and in being able to be yourself. It is a confidence often associated with the young or of the youthful spirit. Fear is not part of the picture. But many of us, poets included, can struggle with self-doubt. There are often significant obstacles, internal or external, to overcome. In these circumstances, confidence is hard-won. Maya Angelou captures that sense of determination in her anthem-poem 'Still I Rise'. She writes, 'You may tread me in the very dirt / But still, like dust, I'll rise' and 'Up from a past that's rooted in pain / I rise'. Like a mantra, insistently, repeatedly, Angelou tells us 'I rise / I rise / I rise.'

Many poems tell of struggles that threaten to overwhelm yet show how, with courage and self-belief, they can be overcome. It often feels like it is out of these very challenges that bravery and resilience are forged, famously articulated by W E Henley: 'Out of the night that covers me, / Black as the pit from pole to pole, / I thank whatever gods may be / For my unconquerable soul' ('Invictus'). For others, such grit and determination are expressed in the poets' use of negatives, such as Emily Brontë declaring 'No coward soul is mine' or Archibald Lampman writing 'Not to be conquered by the headlong days' ('Outlook'). William Blake's 'I will not cease from Mental Fight' ('Jerusalem') feels both defiant and powerful, a sense of rejecting any obstacles that stand in the way.

But it is not only through individual or lonely struggle that confidence emerges. Poets look to others for help. There are heroes of old whom we can turn to for stories of brave struggle and a conquering spirit, such as Tennyson's *Ulysses* who exhorts his followers to be 'strong in will / To strive, to seek, to find, and not to yield', though we should beware the perils of over-confidence in the example of Icarus whose winged flight is 'unable / To sustain its presumptuous mood' (Ronald Bottrall). For others, faith in God provides the framework within which self-confidence can flourish.

When we require vast amounts of confidence and bravery, to fight a battle, for example, or to wage a war, leaders appeal to a collective sense of belonging and shared purpose to rouse their troops; and this type of appeal requires elevated and impassioned language. Arguably the most famous example of this is the speech Shakespeare writes for his warrior king Henry V ('Once more unto the breach dear friends'). Henry V, leading from the front, exhorts his soldiers that 'when the blast of war blows in our ears, / Then imitate the action of the tiger'. Even off the battlefield, we too can be galvanized into action by this fighting spirit.

Whether we turn to the poets of the past or look to contemporary voices, those with the gift of language – those who are lucky enough to 'walk in the visions of Poesy', as Percy Bysshe Shelley puts it – can transform our inner lives with their words. If we listen attentively, their poems could be as effective at giving us a confidence boost as a friend or self-help coach, or even more impactful. Horace's voice from the 1st century BCE still echoes with his famous words '*carpe diem*' (*Odes*), but we can also find inspiration in the different tone of Mary Oliver's words, 'You only have to let the soft animal of your body / love what it loves' ('Wild Geese'). I believe that by trusting the words of the poems, responding to what they have to offer, you will start to feel yourself fill up with that expansive quality of confidence.

What we hear in this symphony of voices is not only these writers' experiences of confidence and their varied responses to the challenges of life but also an invitation, sometimes an exhortation, for us, their readers, to feel fully alive and to be our true selves. If we search within ourselves as well as in the world around us we surely may uncover what perhaps has always been there – confidence and self-belief – or what we might more simply call *love*:

'what I heard was my whole self
saying and singing what it knew: I can.'
('Variation on a Theme by Rilke', Denise Levertov)

My Own Voice
From *The Prelude*, Book 1

My own voice cheered me, and, far more, the mind's
Internal echo of the imperfect sound;
To both I listened, drawing from them both
A cheerful confidence in things to come.

William Wordsworth (1770–1850)

'I am the master of my fate'

Invictus
William Ernest Henley

Variation on a Theme by Rilke

A certain day became a presence to me;
there it was, confronting me – a sky, air, light:
a being. And before it started to descend
from the height of noon, it leaned over
and struck my shoulder as if with
the flat of a sword, granting me
honor and a task. The day's blow
rang out, metallic – or it was I, a bell awakened,
and what I heard was my whole self
saying and singing what it knew: I can.

Denise Levertov (1923-1997)

Say Not the Struggle Nought Availeth

Say not the struggle nought availeth,
    The labour and the wounds are vain,
The enemy faints not, nor faileth,
    And as things have been they remain.

If hopes were dupes, fears may be liars;
    It may be, in yon smoke concealed,
Your comrades chase e'en now the fliers,
    And, but for you, possess the field.

For while the tired waves, vainly breaking
    Seem here no painful inch to gain,
Far back through creeks and inlets making,
    Comes silent, flooding in, the main.

And not by eastern windows only,
    When daylight comes, comes in the light,
In front the sun climbs slow, how slowly,
    But westward, look, the land is bright!

Arthur Hugh Clough (1819-1861)

Ithaka

As you set out for Ithaka
hope your road is a long one,
full of adventure, full of discovery.
Laistrygonians, Cyclops,
angry Poseidon – don't be afraid of them:
you'll never find things like that on your way
as long as you keep your thoughts raised high,
as long as a rare excitement
stirs your spirit and your body.
Laistrygonians, Cyclops,
wild Poseidon – you won't encounter them
unless you bring them along inside your soul,
unless your soul sets them up in front of you.

Hope your road is a long one.
May there be many summer mornings when,
with what pleasure, what joy,
you enter harbors you're seeing for the first time;
may you stop at Phoenician trading stations
to buy fine things,
mother of pearl and coral, amber and ebony,
sensual perfume of every kind –
as many sensual perfumes as you can;
and may you visit many Egyptian cities
to learn and go on learning from their scholars.

Keep Ithaka always in your mind.
Arriving there is what you're destined for.
But don't hurry the journey at all.
Better if it lasts for years,
so you're old by the time you reach the island,
wealthy with all you've gained on the way,
not expecting Ithaka to make you rich.

Ithaka gave you the marvelous journey.
Without her you wouldn't have set out.
She has nothing left to give you now.

And if you find her poor, Ithaka won't have fooled
    you.
Wise as you will have become, so full of experience,
you'll have understood by then what these Ithakas
    mean.

C P Cavafy (1863–1933)
Translated from the Greek by Edmund Keeley (1928–2022)

Jerusalem

And did those feet in ancient time
Walk upon Englands mountains green:
And was the holy Lamb of God,
On Englands pleasant pastures seen!

And did the Countenance Divine,
Shine forth upon our clouded hills?
And was Jerusalem builded here,
Among these dark Satanic Mills?

Bring me my Bow of burning gold:
Bring me my arrows of desire:
Bring me my Spear: O clouds unfold!
Bring me my Chariot of fire!

I will not cease from Mental Fight,
Nor shall my sword sleep in my hand:
  Till we have built Jerusalem,
In Englands green & pleasant Land.

William Blake (1757-1827)

Will

There is no chance, no destiny, no fate,
   Can circumvent or hinder or control
   The firm resolve of a determined soul.
Gifts count for nothing; will alone is great;
All things give way before it, soon or late.
   What obstacle can stay the mighty force
   Of the sea-seeking river in its course,
Or cause the ascending orb of day to wait?
Each well-born soul must win what it deserves.
Let the fool prate of luck. The fortunate
   Is he whose earnest purpose never swerves,
   Whose slightest action or inaction serves
The one great aim.
   Why, even Death stands still,
And waits an hour sometimes for such a will.

Ella Wheeler Wilcox (1850–1919)

A Winter Ride

Who shall declare the joy of the running!
  Who shall tell of the pleasures of flight!
Springing and spurning the tufts of wild heather,
  Sweeping, wide-winged, through the blue dome
    of light.
Everything mortal has moments immortal,
  Swift and God-gifted, immeasurably bright.

So with the stretch of the white road before me,
  Shining snow crystals rainbowed by the sun,
Fields that are white, stained with long, cool, blue
  shadows,
  Strong with the strength of my horse as we run.
Joy in the touch of the wind and the sunlight!
  Joy! With the vigorous earth I am one.

Amy Lowell (1874–1925)

Roll of thunder, Hear my cry

African American Spiritual

Roll of thunder
Hear my cry
Over the water
Bye and bye
Ole man comin'
Down the line
Whip in hand to
Beat me down
But I ain't
Gonna let him
Turn me around.

'to thine
own self
be true'

Hamlet
William Shakespeare

We never know how high we are

We never know how high we are
   Till we are called to rise;
And then, if we are true to plan,
   Our statures touch the skies –

The Heroism we recite
   Would be a daily thing,
Did not ourselves the Cubits warp
   For fear to be a King –

Emily Dickinson (1830–1886)

No Coward Soul is Mine

No coward soul is mine,
No trembler in the world's storm-troubled sphere:
I see Heaven's glories shine,
And Faith shines equal arming me from Fear

O God within my breast,
Almighty ever-present Deity!
Life, that in me hast rest,
As I Undying Life, have power in Thee!

Vain are the thousand creeds
That move men's hearts, unutterably vain;
Worthless as withered weeds,
Or idlest froth amid the boundless main,

To waken doubt in one
Holding so fast by thy infinity,
So surely anchored on
The steadfast rock of Immortality.

With wide-embracing love
Thy Spirit animates eternal years,
   Pervades and broods above,
Changes, sustains, dissolves, creates and rears.

   Though earth and moon were gone,
And suns and universes ceased to be,
   And Thou wert left alone,
Every Existence would exist in Thee.

   There is not room for Death,
Nor atom that his might could render void:
Thou – Thou art Being and Breath,
And what thou art may never be destroyed.

Emily Brontë (1818–1848)

On Myselfe

Good Heav'n, I thank thee, since it was design'd
I shou'd be fram'd, but of the weaker kinde,
That yet, my Soul, is rescu'd from the Love
Of all those Trifles which their Passions move.
Pleasures, and Praise and Plenty have with me
But their just value. If allow'd they be,
Freely, and thankfully as much I tast,
As will not reason, or Religion waste,
If they're deny'd, I on my selfe can Liue,
And slight those aids, unequal chance does give.
When in the Sun, my wings can be display'd,
And in retirement, I can bless the shade.

Anne Finch, Countess of Winchilsea (1661–1720)

Our doubts are traitors
From *Measure for Measure*, Act I, Scene iv

LUCIO

Our doubts are traitors
And make us lose the good we oft might win
By fearing to attempt.

William Shakespeare (1564–1616)

The Harvest of the Seed

From *Janet's Repentance*

Always, there is seed being sown silently and unseen.
And, everywhere there come sweet flowers
without our foresight or labour.

Nature gives us shadow and blossom and fruit
that spring from no planting of ours.

George Eliot (1819–1880)

The Dawning Day

So here hath been dawning
  Another blue day:
Think, wilt thou let it
  Slip useless away?

Out of Eternity
  This new day is born;
Into Eternity,
  At night, doth return.

Behold it aforetime
  No eyes ever did:
So soon it for ever
  From all eyes is hid.

Here hath been dawning
  Another blue day:
Think wilt thou let it
  Slip useless away?

Thomas Carlyle (1795–1881)

The Call

From our low seat beside the fire
Where we have dozed and dreamed and watched the glow
Or raked the ashes, stopping so
We scarcely saw the sun or rain
Above, or looked much higher
Than this same quiet red or burned-out fire.
To-night we heard a call,
A rattle on the window-pane,
A voice on the sharp air,
And felt a breath stirring our hair,
A flame within us: Something swift and tall
Swept in and out and that was all.
Was it a bright or a dark angel? Who can know?
It left no mark upon the snow,
But suddenly it snapped the chain
Unbarred, flung wide the door
Which will not shut again;
And so we cannot sit here any more.

We must arise and go:
The world is cold without
And dark and hedged about
With mystery and enmity and doubt,
But we must go
Though yet we do not know
Who called, or what marks we shall leave upon the snow.

Charlotte Mew (1869-1928)

The Stare's Nest by My Window

The bees build in the crevices
Of loosening masonry, and there
The mother birds bring grubs and flies.
My wall is loosening; honey-bees,
Come build in the empty house of the stare.
We are closed in, and the key is turned
On our uncertainty; somewhere
A man is killed, or a house burned.
Yet no clear fact to be discerned:
Come build in the empty house of the stare.
A barricade of stone or of wood;
Some fourteen days of civil war:
Last night they trundled down the road
That dead young soldier in his blood:
Come build in the empty house of the stare.
We had fed the heart on fantasies,
The heart's grown brutal from the fare,
More substance in our enmities
Than in our love; O honey-bees,
Come build in the empty house of the stare.

W B Yeats (1865-1939)

A Bag of Tools

Isn't it strange
That princes and kings,
And clowns that caper
In sawdust rings,
And common people
Like you and me
Are builders for eternity?

Each is given a bag of tools,
A shapeless mass,
A book of rules;
And each must make –
Ere life is flown –
A stumbling block
Or a stepping stone.

Robert Lee Sharpe (1872–1951)

Content: but we will leave this paltry land

From *The Jew of Malta*, Act IV, scene ii

ITHAMORE

Content: but we will leave this paltry land,
And sail from hence to Greece, to lovely Greece; –
I'll be thy Jason, thou my golden fleece; –
Where painted carpets o'er the meads are hurled.
And Bacchus' vineyards overspread the world;
Where woods and forests go in goodly green.
I'll be Adonis, thou shalt be Love's Queen; –
The meads, the orchards, and the primrose-lanes.
Instead of sedge and reed, bear sugar-canes.

Christopher Marlowe (1564–1593)

'The world was all before them'

Paradise Lost
John Milton

My beloved spake

From *King James Bible*, The Song of Solomon 2:10-13

My beloved spake, and said unto me, Rise up, my
  love, my fair one, and come away.
For, lo, the winter is past, the rain is over and gone;
The flowers appear on the earth; the time of the
  singing of birds is come, and the voice of the turtle
  is heard in our land;
The fig tree putteth forth her green figs, and the
  vines with the tender grape give a good smell. Arise,
  my love, my fair one, and come away.

The Voice of Spring

I am coming, I am coming!
Hark! the honey bee is humming;
See, the lark is soaring high
In the blue and sunny sky,
And the gnats are on the wing
Wheeling round in airy ring.

Listen! New-born lambs are bleating,
And the cawing rooks are meeting
In the elms – a noisy crowd.
All the birds are singing loud,
And the first white butterfly
In the sunshine dances by.

Look around you, look around!
Flowers in all the fields abound,
Every running stream is bright,
All the orchard trees are white,
And each small and waving shoot
Promises sweet autumn fruit.

Mary Howitt (1799–1888)

The time that my journey takes
Gitanjali 12

The time that my journey takes is long and the way
  of it long.
    I came out on the chariot of the first gleam of
      light, and pursued my voyage through the
      wildernesses of worlds leaving my track on many
      a star and planet.
    It is the most distant course that comes nearest
      to thyself, and that training is the most intricate
      which leads to the utter simplicity of a tune.
    The traveller has to knock at every alien door to
      come to his own, and one has to wander through
      all the outer worlds to reach the innermost shrine
      at the end.
    My eyes strayed far and wide before I shut them
      and said 'Here art thou!'
    The question and the cry 'Oh, where?' melt into
      tears of a thousand
streams and deluge the world with the flood of the
  assurance 'I am!'

Rabindranath Tagore (1861–1941)

Ballad of The Tempest

We were crowded in the cabin,
  Not a soul would dare to sleep, –
It was midnight on the waters,
  And a storm was on the deep.

’Tis a fearful thing in winter
  To be shattered by the blast,
And to hear the rattling trumpet
  Thunder, ‘Cut away the mast!’

So we shuddered there in silence, –
  For the stoutest held his breath,
While the hungry sea was roaring,
  And the breakers talked with Death.

As thus we sat in darkness
  Each one busy in his prayers,
‘We are lost!’ the captain shouted,
  As he staggered down the stairs.

But his little daughter whispered,
   As she took his icy hand,
'Isn't God upon the ocean,
   Just the same as on the land?'

Then we kissed the little maiden,
   And we spake in better cheer,
And we anchored safe in harbor
   When the morn was shining clear.

James Thomas Fields (1817–1881)

Pibroch of Donuil Dhu

Pibroch* of Donuil Dhu,
  Pibroch of Donuil,
Wake thy wild voice anew,
  Summon Clan Conuil.
Come away, come away,
  Hark to the summons!
Come in your war array,
  Gentles and commons.

Come from deep glen, and
  From mountain so rocky,
The war-pipe and pennon
  Are at Inverlochy.
Come every hill-plaid, and
  True heart that wears one,
Come every steel blade, and
  Strong hand that bears one.

Leave untended the herd,
  The flock without shelter;
Leave the corpse uninterr'd,
  The bride at the altar;
Leave the deer, leave the steer,
  Leave nets and barges:
Come with your fighting gear,
  Broadswords and targes.

Come as the winds come, when
    Forests are rended;
Come as the waves come, when
    Navies are stranded:
Faster come, faster come,
    Faster and faster,
Chief, vassal, page and groom,
    Tenant and master.

Fast they come, fast they come;
    See how they gather!
Wide waves the eagle plume,
Blended with heather.
Cast your plaids, draw your blades,
    Forward each man set!
Pibroch of Donuil Dhu,
    Knell for the onset!

Sir Walter Scott (1771-1832)
*Music of the Scottish bagpipes

Different

Not to say what everyone else was saying
not to believe what everyone else believed
not to do what everyone else did,
then to refute what everyone else was saying
then to disprove what everyone else believed
then to deprecate what everybody did,

was his way to come by understanding

how everyone else was saying the same as he was
  saying
believing what he believed
and did what doing.

Clere Parsons (1908–1931)

May, 1915

Let us remember Spring will come again
To the scorched, blackened woods, where all the
    wounded trees
Wait, with their old wise patience for the heavenly
    rain,
Sure of the sky: sure of the sea to send its healing
  breeze,
Sure of the sun. And even as to these
Surely the Spring, when God shall please
Will come again like a divine surprise
To those who sit to-day with their great Dead, hands
  in their hands, eyes in their eyes,
At one with Love, at one with Grief: blind to the
  scattered things and changing skies.

Charlotte Mew (1869–1928)

'all forward together!'

'We as Women'
Charlotte Perkins Gilman

Progress

Let there be many windows to your soul,
That all the glory of the universe
May beautify it. Not the narrow pane
Of one poor creed can catch the radiant rays
That shine from countless sources. Tear away
The blinds of superstition; let the light
Pour through fair windows broad as Truth itself
And high as God.

       Why should the spirit peer
Through some priest-curtained orifice, and grope
Along dim corridors of doubt, when all
The splendour from unfathomed seas of space
Might bathe it with the golden waves of Love?
Sweep up the débris of decaying faiths;
Sweep down the cobwebs of worn-out beliefs,
And throw your soul wide open to the light
Of Reason and of Knowledge. Tune your ear
To all the wordless music of the stars
And to the voice of Nature, and your heart
Shall turn to truth and goodness, as the plant
Turns to the sun. A thousand unseen hands
Reach down to help you to their peace-crowned heights,
And all the forces of the firmament
Shall fortify your strength. Be not afraid
To thrust aside half-truths and grasp the whole.

Ella Wheeler Wilcox (1850–1919)

The Monkey's Cousin

I shall reach up, I shall grow
Till the high gods say – Hello,
Little brother, you must stop
Ere our shoulders you o'ertop. –

I shall grow up, I shall reach
Till the little gods beseech
– Master, wait a little, do,
We are running after you! –

I shall bulk and swell and scale
Till the little gods shall quail,
Running everywhere to hide
From the terror of my stride!

James Stephens (1880-1950)

'Firm as a rock thy purpose be'

Restless as billows of the sea
James Henry

Boldness be my friend

From *Cymbeline*, Act I, scene vi

IACHIMO

Boldness be my friend!
Arm me, audacity, from head to foot!

William Shakespeare (1564–1616)

O brave new world
From *The Tempest*, Act V, Scene i

MIRANDA

O, wonder!
How many goodly creatures are there here!
How beauteous mankind is! O brave new world,
That has such people in't!

William Shakespeare (1564–1616)

I Celebrate myself
From *Song of Myself,* 1 (1892 edition)

I Celebrate myself, and sing myself,
And what I assume you shall assume,
For every atom belonging to me as good belongs to
  you.

I loafe and invite my soul,
I lean and loafe at my ease observing a spear of
  summer grass.

My tongue, every atom of my blood, form'd from
  this soil, this air,
Born here of parents born here from parents the
  same, and their parents the same,
I, now thirty-seven years old in perfect health begin,
Hoping to cease not till death.

Creeds and schools in abeyance,
Retiring back a while sufficed at what they are, but
  never forgotten,
I harbor for good or bad, I permit to speak at every
  hazard,
Nature without check with original energy.

Walt Whitman (1819–1892)

Solitude

Laugh, and the world laughs with you;
   Weep, and you weep alone,
For the sad old earth must borrow its mirth,
   But has trouble enough of its own.
Sing, and the hills will answer;
   Sigh, it is lost on the air;
The echoes bound to a joyful sound,
   But shrink from voicing care.

Rejoice, and men will seek you;
   Grieve, and they turn and go.
They want full measure of all your pleasure,
   But they do not need your woe.
Be glad, and your friends are many;
   Be sad, and you lose them all, –
There are none to decline your nectar'd wine,
   But alone you must drink life's gall.

Feast, and your halls are crowded;
   Fast, and the world goes by.
Succeed and give, and it helps you live,
   But no man can help you die.
There is room in the halls of pleasure
   For a large and lordly train,
But one by one we must all file on
   Through the narrow aisles of pain.

Ella Wheeler Wilcox (1850–1919)

'I am myself at last'

I am Like a Rose
D H Lawrence

A Coat

I made my song a coat
Covered with embroideries
Out of old mythologies
From heel to throat;
But the fools caught it,
Wore it in the world's eyes
As though they'd wrought it.
Song, let them take it
For there's more enterprise
In walking naked.

W B Yeats (1865–1939)

Where the mind is without fear
Gitanjali 35

Where the mind is without fear and the head is
  held high;
   Where knowledge is free;
   Where the world has not been broken up into
      fragments by narrow domestic walls
   Where words come out from the depth of truth;
   Where tireless striving stretches its arms towards
      perfection;
   Where the clear stream of reason has not lost its
      way into the dreary desert sand of dead habit;
   Where the mind is led forward by thee into ever-
      widening thought and action –
   Into that heaven of freedom, my Father, let my
      country awake.

Rabindranath Tagore (1861–1941)

Song of a Man Who Has Come Through

Not I, not I, but the wind that blows through me!
A fine wind is blowing the new direction of Time.
If only I let it bear me, carry me, if only it carry me!
If only I am sensitive, subtle, oh, delicate, a winged gift!
If only, most lovely of all, I yield myself and am
  borrowed
By the fine, fine wind that takes its course though the
  chaos of the world
Like a fine, and exquisite chisel, a wedge-blade inserted;
If only I am keen and hard like the sheer tip of a
  wedge
Driven by invisible blows,
The rock will split, we shall come at the wonder, we
  shall find the Hesperides.

Oh, for the wonder that bubbles into my soul,
I would be a good fountain, a good well-head,
Would blur no whisper, spoil no expression.

What is the knocking?
What is the knocking at the door in the night?
It's somebody wants to do us harm.

No, no, it is the three strange angels.
Admit them, admit them.

D H Lawrence (1885-1930)

High Waving Heather

High waving heather, 'neath stormy blasts bending,
  Midnight and moonlight and bright shining stars;
Darkness and glory rejoicingly blending,
Earth rising to heaven and heaven descending,
Man's spirit away from its drear dungeon sending, –
  Bursting the fetters and breaking the bars.

All down the mountain-sides, wild forest lending
  One mighty voice to the life-giving wind;
Rivers their banks in the jubilee rending,
Fast through the valleys a reckless course wending,
Wider and deeper their waters extending,
  Leaving a desolate desert behind.

Shining and lowering and swelling and dying, –
  Changing for ever from midnight to noon;
Roaring like thunder, like soft music sighing,
Shadows on shadows advancing and flying
Lightning-bright flashes the deep gloom defying,
  Coming as swiftly and fading as soon.

Emily Brontë (1818-1848)

Nature, that fram'd us of four elements

From *Tamburlaine the Great*, Part I, Act II, scene vi

Nature, that fram'd us of four elements
Warring within our breasts for regiment.
Doth teach us all to have aspiring minds:
Our souls, whose faculties can comprehend
The wondrous architecture of the world,
And measure every wandering planet's course.
Still climbing after knowledge infinite,
And always moving as the restless spheres.

Christopher Marlowe (1564–1593)

The Windhover
To Christ our Lord

I caught this morning morning's minion, king-
    dom of daylight's dauphin, dapple-dawn-drawn
      Falcon, in his riding
    Of the rolling level underneath him steady air,
      and striding
High there, how he rung upon the rein of a wimpling
    wing
In his ecstasy! then off, off forth on swing,
    As a skate's heel sweeps smooth on a bow-bend:
      the hurl and gliding
    Rebuffed the big wind. My heart in hiding
Stirred for a bird, – the achieve of, the mastery of
    the thing!

Brute beauty and valour and act, oh, air, pride,
    plume, here
    Buckle! AND the fire that breaks from thee then, a
      billion
Times told lovelier, more dangerous, O my chevalier!

    No wonder of it: shéer plód makes plough down
      sillion
Shine, and blue-bleak embers, ah my dear,
    Fall, gall themselves, and gash gold-vermilion.

Gerard Manley Hopkins (1844-1889)

'live in
pulses
stirred to
generosity'

O May I join the choir invisible
George Eliot

To suffer woes which Hope thinks infinite
From *Prometheus Unbound*, Act IV, lines 570-579

To suffer woes which Hope thinks infinite;
To forgive wrongs darker than death or night;
   To defy Power, which seems omnipotent;
To love, and bear; to hope till Hope creates
From its own wreck the thing it contemplates;
   Neither to change, nor falter, nor repent;
This, like thy glory, Titan, is to be
Good, great and joyous, beautiful and free;
This is alone Life; Joy, Empire, and Victory!

Percy Bysshe Shelley (1792–1822)

Outlook

Not to be conquered by these headlong days,
   But to stand free: to keep the mind at brood
   On life's deep meaning, nature's altitude
Of loveliness, and time's mysterious ways;
At every thought and deed to clear the haze
   Out of our eyes, considering only this,
   What man, what life, what love, what beauty is,
This is to live, and win the final praise.

Though strife, ill fortune, and harsh human need
   Beat down the soul, at moments blind and dumb
   With agony; yet patience – there shall come
      Many great voices from life's outer sea,
Hours of strange triumph, and, when few men heed,
   Murmurs and glimpses of eternity.

Archibald Lampman (1861-1899)

God's World

O world, I cannot hold thee close enough!
  Thy winds, thy wide grey skies!
  Thy mists, that roll and rise!
Thy woods, this autumn day, that ache and sag
And all but cry with colour! That gaunt crag
To crush! To lift the lean of that black bluff!
World, World, I cannot get thee close enough!

Long have I known a glory in it all,
  But never knew I this;
  Here such a passion is
As stretcheth me apart, – Lord, I do fear
Thou'st made the world too beautiful this year;
My soul is all but out of me, – let fall
No burning leaf; prithee, let no bird call.

Edna St Vincent Millay (1892–1950)

Come, my friends
From *Ulysses*, lines 56–70

                    Come, my friends,
'Tis not too late to seek a newer world.
Push off, and sitting well in order smite
The sounding furrows; for my purpose holds
To sail beyond the sunset, and the baths
Of all the western stars, until I die.
It may be that the gulfs will wash us down:
It may be we shall touch the Happy Isles,
And see the great Achilles, whom we knew.
Tho' much is taken, much abides; and tho'
We are not now that strength which in old days
Moved earth and heaven, that which we are, we are;
One equal temper of heroic hearts,
Made weak by time and fate, but strong in will
To strive, to seek, to find, and not to yield.

Alfred, Lord Tennyson (1809–1892)

Carpe Diem
From *Odes* 1.11

Tu ne quaesieris, scire nefas, quem mihi, quem tibi
Finem di dederint, Leuconoe, nec Babylonios
Temptaris numeros. Ut melius quidquid erit pati,
Seu pluris hiemes seu tribuit Iuppiter ultimam,
Quae nunc oppositis debilitat pumicibus mare
Tyrrhenum: sapias, vina liques, et spatio brevi
Spem longam reseces. Dum loquimur, fugerit invida
Aetas: carpe diem, quam minimum credula postero.

Ask not ('tis forbidden knowledge), what our destined
  term of years,
Mine and yours; nor scan the tables of your
  Babylonish seers.
Better far to bear the future, my Leuconoe, like the
  past,
Whether Jove has many winters yet to give, or this
  our last;
This, that makes the Tyrrhene billows spend their
  strength against the shore.
Strain your wine and prove your wisdom; life is short;
  should hope be more?
In the moment of our talking, envious time has ebb'd
  away.
Seize the present; trust tomorrow e'en as little as you
  may.

Horace (65 BCE–8 BCE)
Translated from the Latin by John Conington (1825–1869)

When I set out for Lyonnesse

When I set out for Lyonnesse,
  A hundred miles away,
   The rime was on the spray,
And starlight lit my lonesomeness
When I set out for Lyonnesse
      A hundred miles away.

What would bechance at Lyonnesse
While I should sojourn there
  No prophet durst declare,
Nor did the wisest wizard guess
What would bechance at Lyonnesse
  While I should sojourn there.

When I came back from Lyonnesse
  With magic in my eyes,
  All marked with mute surmise
My radiance rare and fathomless,
When I came back from Lyonnesse
  With magic in my eyes!

Thomas Hardy (1840–1928)

Call Letters: Mrs. V.B.

Ships?
Sure I'll sail them
Show me the boat,
If it'll float,
I'll sail it.

Men?
Yes, I'll love them.
If they've got style,
to make me smile,
I'll love them.

Life?
'Course I'll live it.
Just enough breath,
Until my death,
And I'll live it.

Failure?
I'm not ashamed to tell it,
I've never learned to spell it,
Not Failure.

Maya Angelou (1928–2014)

I Hear America Singing

I hear America singing, the varied carols I hear,
Those of mechanics, each one singing his as it should
 be blithe and strong,
The carpenter singing his as he measures his plank
 or beam,
The mason singing his as he makes ready for work,
 or leaves off work,
The boatman singing what belongs to him in his
 boat, the deckhand singing on the steamboat deck,
The shoemaker singing as he sits on his bench, the
 hatter singing as he stands,
The wood-cutter's song, the ploughboy's on his
 way in the morning, or at noon intermission or at
 sundown,
The delicious singing of the mother, or of the young
 wife at work, or of the girl sewing or washing,
Each singing what belongs to him or her and to none
 else,
The day what belongs to the day – at night the party
 of young fellows, robust, friendly,
Singing with open mouths their strong melodious
 songs.

Walt Whitman (1819–1892)

Restless as billows of the sea

Restless as billows of the sea
  And agile be thy feet,
Firm as a rock thy purpose be,
  Nor from the right retreat.

Walking from Schonau to Lichtenstein (Saxony),
 June 19, 1854

James Henry (1798-1876)

His legs bestrid the ocean

From *Antony and Cleopatra*, Act V, Scene ii

CLEOPATRA (On Antony)

His legs bestrid the ocean, his reared arm
Crested the world. His voice was propertied
As all the tunèd spheres, and that to friends;
But when he meant to quail and shake the orb,
He was as rattling thunder. For his bounty,
There was no winter in't; an autumn 'twas
That grew the more by reaping. His delights
Were dolphin-like; they showed his back above
The element they lived in. In his livery
Walked crowns and crownets; realms and islands
  were
As plates dropped from his pocket.

William Shakespeare (1564–1616)

I dwell in Possibility

I dwell in Possibility –
A fairer House than Prose –
More numerous of Windows –
Superior – for Doors –

Of Chambers as the Cedars –
Impregnable of Eye –
And for an Everlasting Roof
The Gambrels of the Sky –

Of Visitors – the fairest –
For Occupation – This –
The spreading wide my narrow Hands
To gather Paradise –

Emily Dickinson (1830-1886)

'Boldness be my friend!'

Cymbeline
William Shakespeare

O May I join the choir invisible

O May I join the choir invisible
Of those immortal dead who live again
In minds made better by their presence: live
In pulses stirred to generosity,
In deeds of daring rectitude, in scorn
For miserable aims that end with self,
In thoughts sublime that pierce the night like stars,
And with their mild persistence urge man's search
To vaster issues.

          So to live is heaven:
To make undying music in the world,
Breathing as beauteous order that controls
With growing sway the growing life of man.
So we inherit that sweet purity
For which we struggled, failed, and agonized
With widening retrospect that bred despair.
Rebellious flesh that would not be subdued,
A vicious parent shaming still its child,
Poor anxious penitence, is quick dissolved;
Its discords, quenched by meeting harmonies,
Die in the large and charitable air.
And all our rarer, better, truer self,
That sobbed religiously in yearning song,
That watched to ease the burthen of the world,
Laboriously tracing what must be,
And what may yet be better, – saw within

A worthier image for the sanctuary,
And shaped it forth before the multitude,
Divinely human, raising worship so
To higher reverence more mixed with love, –
That better self shall live till human Time
Shall fold its eyelids, and the human sky
Be gathered like a scroll within the tomb
Unread forever.
                    This is life to come,
Which martyred men have made more glorious
For us who strive to follow. May I reach
That purest heaven, be to other souls
The cup of strength in some great agony,
Enkindle generous ardor, feed pure love,
Beget the smiles that have no cruelty –
Be the sweet presence of a good diffused,
And in diffusion ever more intense!
So shall I join the choir invisible
Whose music is the gladness of the world.

George Eliot (1819-1880)

Wild Geese

You do not have to be good.
You do not have to walk on your knees
For a hundred miles through the desert, repenting.
You only have to let the soft animal of your body
love what it loves.
Tell me about despair, yours, and I will tell you mine.
Meanwhile the world goes on.
Meanwhile the sun and the clear pebbles of the rain
are moving across the landscapes,
over the prairies and the deep trees,
the mountains and the rivers.
Meanwhile the wild geese, high in the clean blue air,
are heading home again.
Whoever you are, no matter how lonely,
the world offers itself to your imagination,
calls to you like the wild geese, harsh and exciting –
over and over announcing your place
in the family of things.

Mary Oliver (1935–2019)

A Birthday

My heart is like a singing bird
   Whose nest is in a watered shoot;
My heart is like an apple-tree
   Whose boughs are bent with thick-set fruit;
My heart is like a rainbow shell
   That paddles in a halcyon sea;
My heart is gladder than all these
   Because my love is come to me.

Raise me a dais of silk and down;
   Hang it with vair and purple dyes;
Carve it in doves and pomegranates,
   And peacocks with a hundred eyes;
Work it in gold and silver grapes,
   In leaves and silver fleurs-de-lys;
Because the birthday of my life
   Is come, my love is come to me.

Christina Rossetti (1830–1894)

Lines Composed in a Wood
on a Windy Day

My soul is awakened, my spirit is soaring
   And carried aloft on the winds of the breeze;
For above and around me the wild wind is roaring,
   Arousing to rapture the earth and the seas.

The long withered grass in the sunshine is glancing,
   The bare trees are tossing their branches on high;
The dead leaves beneath them are merrily dancing,
   The white clouds are scudding across the blue sky.

I wish I could see how the ocean is lashing
   The foam of its billows to whirlwinds of spray;
I wish I could see how its proud waves are dashing,
   And hear the wild roar of their thunder to-day!

Anne Brontë (1820–1849)

Life

Let me but live my life from year to year,
    With forward face and unreluctant soul;
    Not hurrying to, nor turning from, the goal;
Not mourning for the things that disappear
In the dim past, nor holding back in fear
    From what the future veils; but with a whole
    And happy heart, that pays its toll
To Youth and Age, and travels on with cheer.

So let the way wind up the hill or down,
    O'er rough or smooth, the journey will be joy:
    Still seeking what I sought when but a boy,
New friendship, high adventure, and a crown,
My heart will keep the courage of the quest,
And hope the road's last turn will be the best.

Henry Van Dyke (1852–1933)

Invictus

Out of the night that covers me,
  Black as the pit from pole to pole,
I thank whatever gods may be
  For my unconquerable soul.

In the fell clutch of circumstance
  I have not winced nor cried aloud.
Under the bludgeonings of chance
  My head is bloody, but unbowed.

Beyond this place of wrath and tears
  Looms but the Horror of the shade,
And yet the menace of the years
  Finds and shall find me unafraid.

It matters not how strait the gate,
  How charged with punishments the scroll,
I am the master of my fate:
  I am the captain of my soul.

William Ernest Henley (1849–1903)

Right's Security

What if the wind do howl without,
And turn the creaking weather-vane;
What if the arrows of the rain
Do beat against the window-pane?
Art thou not armored strong and fast
Against the sallies of the blast?
Art thou not sheltered safe and well
Against the flood's insistent swell?

What boots it, that thou stand'st alone,
And laughest in the battle's face
When all the weak have fled the place
And let their feet and fears keep pace?
Thou wavest still thine ensign, high,
And shoutest thy loud battle-cry;
Higher than e'er the tempest roared,
It cleaves the silence like a sword.

Right arms and armors, too, that man
Who will not compromise with wrong;
Though single, he must front the throng,
And wage the battle hard and long.
Minorities, since time began,
Have shown the better side of man;
And often in the lists of Time
One man has made a cause sublime!

Paul Laurence Dunbar (1872-1906)

Young Genius
Extract

If thou wouldst win a lasting fame;
If thou the immortal wreath wouldst claim.
And make the Future bless thy name;

Begin thy perilous career; –
Keep high thy heart, thy conscience clear; –
And walk thy way without a fear.

And if thou hast a voice within,
That ever whispers – 'Work and win,'
And keeps thy soul from sloth and sin:

If thou canst plan a noble deed,
And never flag till it succeed,
Though in the strife thy heart should bleed:

If thou canst struggle day and night,
And in the envious world's despite,
Still keep thy cynosure in sight:

If thou canst bear the rich man's scorn,
Nor curse the day that thou wert born,
To feed on husks, and he on corn:

If thou canst dine upon a crust,
And still hold on with patient trust.
Nor pine that Fortune is unjust:

If thou canst see, with tranquil breast,
The knave or fool in purple dress'd,
Whilst thou must walk in tatter'd vest:

If thou canst rise ere break of day,
And toil and moil till evening gray,
At thankless work, for scanty pay:

If in thy progress to renown,
Thou canst endure the scoff and frown
Of those who strive to pull thee down:

If thou canst bear the averted face,
The gibe, or treacherous embrace,
Of those who run the selfsame race:

If thou in darkest days canst find
An inner brightness in thy mind.
To reconcile thee to thy kind: –

Whatever obstacles control,
Thine hour will come – go on, true soul!
Thoul't win the prize, thoul't reach the goal.

If not – what matters? tried by fire,
And purified from low desire,
Thy spirit shall but soar the higher.

Content and hope thy heart shall buoy,
And men's neglect shall ne'er destroy
Thy secret peace, thy inward joy;

And when thou sittest on the height,
Thy song shall be its own delight,
And cheer thee in the world's despite.

Charles Mackay (1814-1889)

I am Like a Rose

I am myself at last; now I achieve
My very self. I, with the wonder mellow,
Full of fine warmth, I issue forth in clear
And single me, perfected from my fellow.

Here I am all myself. No rose-bush heaving
Its limpid sap to culmination has brought
Itself more sheer and naked out of the green
In stark-clear roses, than I to myself am brought.

D H Lawrence (1885-1930)

'My heart will keep the courage'

Life
Henry Van Dyke

Listening

'Tis you that are the music, not your song.
      The song is but a door which, opening wide,
      Lets forth the pent-up melody inside,
Your spirit's harmony, which clear and strong
Sings but of you. Throughout your whole life long
      Your songs, your thoughts, your doings, each
  divide
      This perfect beauty; waves within a tide
Or single notes amid a glorious throng.
      The song of earth has many different chords;
Ocean has many moods and many tones
      Yet always ocean. In the damp Spring woods
The painted trillium smiles, while crisp pine cones
      Autumn alone can ripen. So is this
      One music with a thousand cadences.

Amy Lowell (1874-1925)

It Was an April Morning:
Fresh and Clear

It was an April morning: fresh and clear
The Rivulet, delighting in its strength,
Ran with a young man's speed; and yet the voice
Of waters which the winter had supplied
Was softened down into a vernal tone.
The spirit of enjoyment and desire,
And hopes and wishes, from all living things
Went circling, like a multitude of sounds.
The budding groves seemed eager to urge on
The steps of June; as if their various hues
Were only hindrances that stood between
Them and their object: but, meanwhile, prevailed
Such an entire contentment in the air
That every naked ash, and tardy tree
Yet leafless, showed as if the countenance
With which it looked on this delightful day
Were native to the summer. – Up the brook
I roamed in the confusion of my heart,
Alive to all things and forgetting all.
At length I to a sudden turning came
In this continuous glen, where down a rock
The Stream, so ardent in its course before,
Sent forth such sallies of glad sound, that all
Which I till then had heard, appeared the voice
Of common pleasure: beast and bird, the lamb,

The shepherd's dog, the linnet and the thrush
Vied with this waterfall, and made a song,
Which, while I listened, seemed like the wild growth
Or like some natural produce of the air,
That could not cease to be. Green leaves were here;
But 'twas the foliage of the rocks – the birch,
The yew, the holly, and the bright green thorn,
With hanging islands of resplendent furze:
And, on a summit, distant a short space,
By any who should look beyond the dell,
A single mountain-cottage might be seen.
I gazed and gazed, and to myself I said,
'Our thoughts at least are ours; and this wild nook,
My EMMA, I will dedicate to thee.'
– Soon did the spot become my other home,
My dwelling, and my out-of-doors abode.
And, of the Shepherds who have seen me there,
To whom I sometimes in our idle talk
Have told this fancy, two or three, perhaps,
Years after we are gone and in our graves,
When they have cause to speak of this wild place,
May call it by the name of EMMA'S DELL.

William Wordsworth (1770–1850)

93 Percent Stardust

We have calcium in our bones,
iron in our veins,
carbon in our souls,
and nitrogen in our brains.

93 percent stardust,
with souls made of flames,
we are all just stars
that have people names.

Nikita Gill (b. 1987)

Once more unto the breach, dear friends
From *Henry V*, Act III, Scene i

Once more unto the breach, dear friends, once more;
Or close the wall up with our English dead!
In peace there's nothing so becomes a man
As modest stillness and humility,
But when the blast of war blows in our ears,
Then imitate the action of the tiger:
Stiffen the sinews, summon up the blood,
Disguise fair nature with hard-favoured rage;
Then lend the eye a terrible aspect,
Let it pry through the portage of the head
Like the brass cannon; let the brow o'erwhelm it
As fearfully as doth a gallèd rock
O'erhang and jutty his confounded base
Swilled with the wild and wasteful ocean.
Now set the teeth, and stretch the nostril wide,
Hold hard the breath, and bend up every spirit
To his full height. On, on, you noblest English.

William Shakespeare (1564-1616)

Now I Become Myself

Now I become myself. It's taken
Time, many years and places;
I have been dissolved and shaken,
Worn other people's faces,
Run madly, as if Time were there,
Terribly old, crying a warning,
'Hurry, you will be dead before –'
(What? Before you reach the morning?
Or the end of the poem is clear?
Or love safe in the walled city?)
Now to stand still, to be here,
Feel my own weight and density!
The black shadow on the paper
Is my hand; the shadow of a word
As thought shapes the shaper
Falls heavy on the page, is heard.
All fuses now, falls into place

From wish to action, word to silence,
My work, my love, my time, my face
Gathered into one intense
Gesture of growing like a plant.
As slowly as the ripening fruit
Fertile, detached, and always spent,
Falls but does not exhaust the root,
So all the poem is, can give,
Grows in me to become the song,
Made so and rooted by love.
Now there is time and Time is young.
O, in this single hour I live
All of myself and do not move.
I, the pursued, who madly ran,
Stand still, stand still, and stop the sun!

May Sarton (1912-1995)

Self-Reliance

Henceforth, please God, forever I forego
The yoke of men's opinions. I will be
Light-hearted as a bird, and live with God.
I find him in the bottom of my heart,
I hear continually his voice therein.

The little needle always knows the North,
The little bird remembereth his note,
And this wise Seer within me never errs.
I never taught it what it teaches me;
I only follow, when I act aright.

Ralph Waldo Emerson (1803–1882)

Frederick Douglass

A hush is over all the teeming lists,
   And there is pause, a breath-space in the strife;
A spirit brave has passed beyond the mists
   And vapors that obscure the sun of life.
And Ethiopia, with bosom torn,
Laments the passing of her noblest born.

She weeps for him a mother's burning tears –
   She loved him with a mother's deepest love.
He was her champion thro' direful years,
   And held her weal all other ends above.
When Bondage held her bleeding in the dust,
He raised her up and whispered, 'Hope and Trust.'

For her his voice, a fearless clarion, rung
   That broke in warning on the ears of men;
For her the strong bow of his power he strung,
   And sent his arrows to the very den
Where grim Oppression held his bloody place
And gloated o'er the mis'ries of a race.

And he was no soft-tongued apologist;
   He spoke straightforward, fearlessly uncowed;
The sunlight of his truth dispelled the mist,
   And set in bold relief each dark hued cloud;
To sin and crime he gave their proper hue,
And hurled at evil what was evil's due.

Through good and ill report he cleaved his way.
    Right onward, with his face set toward the heights,
Nor feared to face the foeman's dread array, –
    The lash of scorn, the sting of petty spites.
He dared the lightning in the lightning's track,
And answered thunder with his thunder back.

When men maligned him, and their torrent wrath
    In furious imprecations o'er him broke,
He kept his counsel as he kept his path;
    'Twas for his race, not for himself he spoke.
He knew the import of his Master's call,
And felt himself too mighty to be small.

No miser in the good he held was he, –
    His kindness followed his horizon's rim.
His heart, his talents, and his hands were free
    To all who truly needed aught of him.
Where poverty and ignorance were rife,
He gave his bounty as he gave his life.

The place and cause that first aroused his might
    Still proved its power until his latest day.
In Freedom's lists and for the aid of Right
    Still in the foremost rank he waged the fray;
Wrong lived; his occupation was not gone.
He died in action with his armor on!

We weep for him, but we have touched his hand,
  And felt the magic of his presence nigh,
The current that he sent throughout the land,
  The kindling spirit of his battle-cry.
O'er all that holds us we shall triumph yet,
And place our banner where his hopes were set!

Oh, Douglass, thou hast passed beyond the shore,
  But still thy voice is ringing o'er the gale!
Thou'st taught thy race how high her hopes
 may soar,
  And bade her seek the heights, nor faint, nor fail.
She will not fail, she heeds thy stirring cry,
She knows thy guardian spirit will be nigh,
And, rising from beneath the chast'ning rod,
She stretches out her bleeding hands to God!

Paul Laurence Dunbar (1872-1906)

To his Heart, bidding it have no Fear

Be you still, be you still, trembling heart;
Remember the wisdom out of the old days:
Him who trembles before the flame and the flood,
And the winds that blow through the starry ways,
Let the starry winds and the flame and the flood
Cover over and hide, for he has no part
With the lonely, majestical multitude.

W B Yeats (1865–1939)

'We As Women'

There's a cry in the air about us –
We hear it before, behind –
Of the way in which 'We, as women,'
Are going to lift mankind!

With our white frocks starched and ruffled,
And our soft hair brushed and curled –
Hats off! for 'We, as women,'
Are coming to save the world.

Fair sisters, listen one moment –
And perhaps you'll pause for ten:
The business of women as women
Is only with men as men!

What we do, 'We, as women,'
We have done all through our life;
The work that is ours as women
Is the work of mother and wife.

But to elevate public opinion,
And to lift up erring man,
Is the work of the Human Being;
Let us do it – if we can.

But wait, warm-hearted sisters –
Not quite so fast, so far.
Tell me how we are going to lift a thing
Any higher than we are!

We are going to 'purify politics,'
And to 'elevate the press.'
We enter the foul paths of the world
To sweeten and cleanse and bless.

To hear the high things we are going to do,
And the horrors of man we tell,
One would think, 'We, as women,' were angels,
And our brothers were fiends of hell.

We, that were born of one mother,
And reared in the selfsame place,
In the school and the church together,
We of one blood, one race!

Now then, all forward together!
But remember, every one,
That 'tis not by feminine innocence
The work of the world is done.

The world needs strength and courage,
And wisdom to help and feed –
When, 'We, as women' bring these to man,
We shall lift the world indeed.

Charlotte Perkins Gilman (1860–1935)

'to hope
till Hope
creates'

Prometheus Unbound
Percy Bysshe Shelley

Still I Rise

You may write me down in history
With your bitter, twisted lies,
You may tread me in the very dirt
But still, like dust, I'll rise.

Does my sassiness upset you?
Why are you beset with gloom?
'Cause I walk like I've got oil wells
Pumping in my living room.

Just like moons and like suns,
With the certainty of tides,
Just like hopes springing high,
Still I'll rise.

Did you want to see me broken?
Bowed head and lowered eyes?
Shoulders falling down like teardrops.
Weakened by my soulful cries.

Does my haughtiness offend you?
Don't you take it awful hard
'Cause I laugh like I've got gold mines
Diggin' in my own back yard.

You may shoot me with your words,
You may cut me with your eyes,
You may kill me with your hatefulness,
But still, like air, I'll rise.

Does my sexiness upset you?
Does it come as a surprise
That I dance like I've got diamonds
At the meeting of my thighs?

Out of the huts of history's shame
I rise
Up from a past that's rooted in pain
I rise
I'm a black ocean, leaping and wide,
Welling and swelling I bear in the tide.
Leaving behind nights of terror and fear
I rise
Into a daybreak that's wondrously clear
I rise
Bringing the gifts that my ancestors gave,
I am the dream and the hope of the slave.
I rise
I rise
I rise.

Maya Angelou (1928–2014)

Speech to the Young:
Speech to the Progress-Toward
(Among them Nora and Henry III)

Say to them,
say to the down-keepers,
the sun-slappers,
the self-soilers,
the harmony-hushers,
'Even if you are not ready for day
it cannot always be night.'
You will be right.
For that is the hard home-run.

Live not for battles won.
Live not for the-end-of-the-song.
Live in the along.

Gwendolyn Brooks (1917–2000)

Craving for Spring
Extract

Ah come, come quickly, spring!
Come and lift us towards our culmination, we
      myriads;
we who have never flowered, like patient cactuses.
Come and lift us to our end, to blossom, bring us
      to our summer
we who are winter-weary in the winter of the
    world.
Come making the chaffinch nests hollow and cosy,
come and soften the willow buds till they are
      puffed and furred,
then blow them over with gold.
Come and cajole the gawky colt's-foot flowers.

Come quickly, and vindicate us
against too much death.
Come quickly, and stir the rotten globe of the
      world from within,
burst it with germination, with world anew.
Come now, to us, your adherents, who cannot
      flower from the ice.
All the world gleams with the lilies of Death the
      Unconquerable,
but come, give us our turn.
Enough of the virgins and lilies, of passionate,
      suffocating perfume of corruption,

no more narcissus perfume, lily harlots, the blades
     of sensation
piercing the flesh to blossom of death.
Have done, have done with this shuddering,
     delicious business
of thrilling ruin in the flesh, of pungent passion,
     of rare, death-edged ecstasy.
Give us our turn, give us a chance, let our hour
     strike,
O soon, soon!

Let the darkness turn violet with rich dawn.
Let the darkness be warmed, warmed through
   to a ruddy violet,
incipient purpling towards summer in the world
     of the heart of man.

Are the violets already here!
Show me! I tremble so much to hear it, that
   even now
on the threshold of spring, I fear I shall die.
Show me the violets that are out.

Oh, if it be true, and the living darkness of the
        blood of man is purpling with violets,
if the violets are coming out from under the rack
        of men, winter-rotten and fallen
we shall have spring.
Pray not to die on this Pisgah blossoming with
        violets.
Pray to live through.

If you catch a whiff of violets from the darkness
    of the shadow of man
it will be spring in the world,
it will be spring in the world of the living;
wonderment organising itself, heralding itself with
        the violets,
stirring of new seasons.

Ah, do not let me die on the brink of such
        anticipation!
Worse, let me not deceive myself.

D H Lawrence (1885-1930)

Keep Going

When things go wrong, as they sometimes will,
And the road you're trudging seems all uphill,
When the funds are low and the debts are high,
And you want to smile, but you have to sigh,
When care is pressing you down a bit,
Rest if you must, but don't you quit.
Life is queer with its twists and turns,
As every one of us sometimes learns.
And many a failure turns about
When he might have won had he stuck it out.
Don't give up though the pace seems slow,
You may succeed with another blow.
Often the goal is nearer than it seems
To a faint and faltering man.
Often the struggler has given up when he
Might have captured the victor's cup,
And he learned too late when the night slipped down,
How close he was to the golden crown.
Success is failure turned inside out,
The silver tint of the clouds of doubt,
And you never can tell how close you are.
It may be near when it seems afar.
So stick to the fight when you're hardest hit.
It's when things seem worst that
You mustn't quit.

Edgar Albert Guest (1881-1959)

Joy

Joy shakes me like the wind that lifts a sail,
Like the roistering wind
That laughs through stalwart pines.
It floods me like the sun
On rain-drenched trees
That flash with silver and green.

I abandon myself to joy –
I laugh – I sing.
Too long have I walked a desolate way,
Too long stumbled down a maze
Bewildered.

Clarissa Scott Delany (1901–1927)

The World
Extract

I saw Eternity the other night,
Like a great ring of pure and endless light,
   All calm, as it was bright;
And round beneath it, Time in hours, days, years,
   Driv'n by the spheres
Like a vast shadow mov'd; in which the world
   And all her train were hurl'd.

Henry Vaughan (1621–1695)

'My own voice cheered me'

The Prelude
William Wordsworth

The Character of a Happy Life

How happy is he born and taught
That serveth not another's will;
Whose armour is his honest thought,
And simple truth his utmost skill!

Whose passions not his masters are;
Whose soul is still prepared for death,
Untied unto the world by care
Of public fame or private breath;

Who envies none that chance doth raise,
Nor vice; who never understood
How deepest wounds are given by praise;
Nor rules of state, but rules of good;

Who hath his life from rumours freed;
Whose conscience is his strong retreat;
Whose state can neither flatterers feed,
Nor ruin make oppressors great;

Who God doth late and early pray
More of His grace than gifts to lend;
And entertains the harmless day
With a religious book or friend;

– This man is freed from servile bands
Of hope to rise or fear to fall:
Lord of himself, though not of lands,
And having nothing, yet hath all.

Sir Henry Wotton (1568-1639)

The world was all before them
From *Paradise Lost*, Book XII

In either hand the hastening Angel caught
Our lingering parents, and to the eastern gate
Led them direct, and down the cliff as fast
To the subjected plain; then disappeared.
They, looking back, all the eastern side beheld
Of Paradise, so late their happy seat,
Waved over by that flaming brand; the gate
With dreadful faces thronged, and fiery arms:
Some natural tears they dropt, but wiped them soon;
The world was all before them, where to choose
Their place of rest, and Providence their guide:
They, hand in hand, with wandering steps and slow,
Through Eden took their solitary way.

John Milton (1608-1674)

We two boys together clinging

We two boys together clinging,
One the other never leaving,
Up and down the roads going, North and South
  excursions making,
Power enjoying, elbows stretching, fingers clutching,
Arm'd and fearless, eating, drinking, sleeping, loving,
No law less than ourselves owning, sailing, soldiering,
  thieving, threatening,
Misers, menials, priests alarming, air breathing, water
  drinking, on the turf or the sea-beach dancing,
Cities wrenching, ease scorning, statutes mocking,
  feebleness chasing,
Fulfilling our foray.

Walt Whitman (1819-1892)

Fern Hill

Now as I was young and easy under the apple boughs
About the lilting house and happy as the grass was
  green,
    The night above the dingle starry,
        Time let me hail and climb
    Golden in the heydays of his eyes,
And honoured among wagons I was prince of the
  apple towns
And once below a time I lordly had the trees and
  leaves
        Trail with daisies and barley
    Down the rivers of the windfall light.

And as I was green and carefree, famous among
  the barns
About the happy yard and singing as the farm was
  home,
    In the sun that is young once only,
        Time let me play and be
    Golden in the mercy of his means,
And green and golden I was huntsman and
  herdsman, the calves
Sang to my horn, the foxes on the hills barked clear
  and cold,
        And the sabbath rang slowly
    In the pebbles of the holy streams.

All the sun long it was running, it was lovely, the hay
Fields high as the house, the tunes from the
   chimneys, it was air
      And playing, lovely and watery
            And fire green as grass.
      And nightly under the simple stars
As I rode to sleep the owls were bearing the farm
   away,
All the moon long I heard, blessed among stables,
   the nightjars
      Flying with the ricks, and the horses
            Flashing into the dark.

And then to awake, and the farm, like a wanderer
   white
With the dew, come back, the cock on his shoulder:
   it was all
      Shining, it was Adam and maiden,
            The sky gathered again
      And the sun grew round that very day.
So it must have been after the birth of the simple light
In the first, spinning place, the spellbound horses
   walking warm
      Out of the whinnying green stable
            On to the fields of praise.

And honoured among foxes and pheasants by the
  gay house
Under the new made clouds and happy as the heart
  was long,
   In the sun born over and over,
      I ran my heedless ways,
   My wishes raced through the house high hay
And nothing I cared, at my sky blue trades, that time
  allows
In all his tuneful turning so few and such morning songs
   Before the children green and golden
      Follow him out of grace,

Nothing I cared, in the lamb white days, that time
  would take me
Up to the swallow thronged loft by the shadow of
  my hand,
   In the moon that is always rising,
      Nor that riding to sleep
   I should hear him fly with the high fields
And wake to the farm forever fled from the childless land.
Oh as I was young and easy in the mercy of his means,
      Time held me green and dying
   Though I sang in my chains like the sea.

Dylan Thomas (1914–1953)

The Masque of Anarchy
Extract

I

As I lay asleep in Italy,
There came a voice from over the Sea,
And with great power it forth led me
To walk in the visions of Poesy.
…

XXXVII

'Men of England, Heirs of Glory,
Heroes of unwritten story,
Nurslings of one mighty mother,
Hopes of her, and one another,
…

XCI

'Rise like lions after slumber
In unvanquishable number!
Shake your chains to earth like dew
Which in sleep had fall'n on you:
Ye are many – they are few.'

Percy Bysshe Shelley (1792-1822)

I Know My Soul

I plucked my soul out of its secret place,
And held it to the mirror of my eye,
To see it like a star against the sky,
A twitching body quivering in space,
A spark of passion shining on my face.
And I explored it to determine why
This awful key to my infinity
Conspires to rob me of sweet joy and grace.
And if the sign may not be fully read,
If I can comprehend but not control,
I need not gloom my days with futile dread,
Because I see a part and not the whole.
Contemplating the strange, I'm comforted
By this narcotic thought: I know my soul.

Claude McKay (1890-1948)

Confidence

Oppressed with sin and woe,
    A burdened heart I bear,
Opposed by many a mighty foe;
    But I will not despair.

With this polluted heart
    I dare to come to Thee,
Holy and mighty as Thou art;
    For Thou wilt pardon me.

I feel that I am weak,
    And prone to every sin:
But Thou who giv'st to those who seek,
    Wilt give me strength within.

Far as this earth may be
    From yonder starry skies;
Remoter still am I from Thee:
    Yet Thou wilt not despise.

I need not fear my foes,
　　I need not yield to care,
I need not sink beneath my woes:
　　For Thou wilt answer prayer.

In my Redeemer's name,
　　I give myself to Thee;
And all unworthy as I am
　　My God will cherish me.

Anne Brontë (1820–1849)

Then I Saw What the Calling Was

All the voices of the wood called 'Muriel!'
But it was soon solved;   it was nothing, it was not
  for me.
The words were a little like Mortal and More and
  Endure
and a word like Real, a sound like Health or Hell.
Then I saw what the calling was   :   it was the
  road I traveled, the clear
time and these colors of orchards, gold behind gold
  and the full
shadow behind each tree and behind each slope. Not
  to me
the calling, but to anyone and at last I saw: where
the road lay through sunlight and many voices and
  the marvel
orchard, not for me, not for me, not for me.
I came into my clear being;   uncalled, alive, and
  sure.
Nothing was speaking to me, but I offered and all
  was well.

And then I arrived at the powerful green hill.

Muriel Rukeyser (1913-1980)

A Mile With Me

O who will walk a mile with me
   Along life's merry way?
A comrade blithe and full of glee,
Who dares to laugh out loud and free,
And let his frolic fancy play,
Like a happy child, through the flowers gay
That fill the field and fringe the way
   Where he walks a mile with me.

And who will walk a mile with me
   Along life's weary way?
A friend whose heart has eyes to see
The stars shine out o'er the darkening lea,
And the quiet rest at the end o' the day, –
A friend who knows, and dares to say,
The brave, sweet words that cheer the way
   Where he walks a mile with me.

With such a comrade, such a friend,
I fain would walk till journeys end,
Through summer sunshine, winter rain,
And then? – Farewell, we shall meet again!

Henry Van Dyke (1852-1933)

'I Celebrate myself'

Song of Myself
Walt Whitman

Oh! pleasant exercise of hope and joy!

From *The Prelude*, Book XI

Oh! pleasant exercise of hope and joy!
For mighty were the auxiliars which then stood
Upon our side, we who were strong in love!
Bliss was it in that dawn to be alive,
But to be young was very heaven!

William Wordsworth (1770–1850)

Life is mostly froth and bubble
From *Finis Exoptatus*

'Question not, but live and labour
 Till yon goal be won,
Helping every feeble neighbour,
Seeking help from none;
Life is mostly froth and bubble,
Two things stand like stone,
KINDNESS in another's trouble,
COURAGE in your own.'

Adam Lindsay Gordon (1833–1870)

The Oak

Live thy Life,
  Young and old,
Like yon oak,
Bright in spring,
  Living gold;

Summer-rich
  Then; and then
Autumn-changed
Soberer-hued
  Gold again.

All his leaves
  Fall'n at length,
Look, he stands,
Trunk and bough
  Naked strength.

Alfred, Lord Tennyson (1809-1892)

A Litany for Survival

For those of us who live at the shoreline
standing upon the constant edges of decision
crucial and alone
for those of us who cannot indulge
the passing dreams of choice
who love in doorways coming and going
in the hours between dawns
looking inward and outward
at once before and after
seeking a now that can breed
futures
like bread in our children's mouths
so their dreams will not reflect
the death of ours;

For those of us
who were imprinted with fear
like a faint line in the center of our foreheads
learning to be afraid with our mother's milk
for by this weapon
this illusion of some safety to be found
the heavy-footed hoped to silence us
For all of us
this instant and this triumph
We were never meant to survive.

And when the sun rises we are afraid
it might not remain
when the sun sets we are afraid
it might not rise in the morning
when our stomachs are full we are afraid
of indigestion
when our stomachs are empty we are afraid
we may never eat again
when we are loved we are afraid
love will vanish
when we are alone we are afraid
love will never return
and when we speak we are afraid
our words will not be heard
nor welcomed
but when we are silent
we are still afraid

So it is better to speak
remembering
we were never meant to survive.

Audre Lorde (1934–1992)

To thine ownself be true

From *Hamlet*, Act I, Scene iii

POLONIUS

The wind sits in the shoulder of your sail,
And you are stay'd for. There; my blessing with thee!
And these few precepts in thy memory
See thou character. Give thy thoughts no tongue,
Nor any unproportioned thought his act.
Be thou familiar, but by no means vulgar.
Those friends thou hast, and their adoption tried,
Grapple them to thy soul with hoops of steel;
But do not dull thy palm with entertainment
Of each new-hatch'd, unfledged comrade. Beware
Of entrance to a quarrel, but being in,
Bear't that the opposed may beware of thee.
Give every man thy ear, but few thy voice;
Take each man's censure, but reserve thy judgment.

Costly thy habit as thy purse can buy,
But not express'd in fancy; rich, not gaudy;
For the apparel oft proclaims the man,
And they in France of the best rank and station
Are of a most select and generous chief in that.
Neither a borrower nor a lender be;
For loan oft loses both itself and friend,
And borrowing dulls the edge of husbandry.
This above all: to thine ownself be true,
And it must follow, as the night the day,
Thou canst not then be false to any man.
Farewell: my blessing season this in thee!

William Shakespeare (1564–1616)

Icarus

In his father's face flying
He soared until the cities of the Aegean
Opened like bloodvessels lying
Under a microscope. End on
He saw below the trunks of trees
While space-time flowered in his sunward eyes.
His feathered arms, extension
Of nimble thoughts, pride of invention,
Were lifting him high above man.
'And if I fly,'
He said, 'to the source of mortal energy
I shall capture the receipt
To administer light and heat.'
But sunlight to all eyes is not bearable
Or sunheat to all blood.
His motion turned to earth, unable
To sustain its presumptuous mood.
Falling he saw the cantilevered birds,

Their great humerus muscles bearing
Them in their spacious veering
Over shores and sherds
Over swords and words.
Like a detached leaf, feeble
In the wind, he fell,
A multitude of molecules
Organized in equal and parallel
Velocities (according to the rules
Of motion) to seek the ground.
And on the slope above the sea
The hard handed-peasants go their round
Turning the soil, blind to the body
Ambitious and viable, whose pride
Will leave no trace in the quenching tide.

Ronald Bottrall (1906-1989)

Courage

It is in the small things we see it.
The child's first step,
as awesome as an earthquake.
The first time you rode a bike,
wallowing up the sidewalk.
The first spanking when your heart
went on a journey all alone.
When they called you crybaby
or poor or fatty or crazy
and made you into an alien,
you drank their acid
and concealed it.

Later,
if you faced the death of bombs and bullets
you did not do it with a banner,
you did it with only a hat to
cover your heart.
You did not fondle the weakness inside you
though it was there.
Your courage was a small coal
that you kept swallowing.
If your buddy saved you
and died himself in so doing,
then his courage was not courage,
it was love; love as simple as shaving soap.

Later,
if you have endured a great despair,
then you did it alone,
getting a transfusion from the fire,
picking the scabs off our heart,
then wringing it out like a sock.
Next, my kinsman, you powdered your sorrow,
you gave it a back rub
and then you covered it with a blanket
and after it had slept a while
it woke to the wings of the roses
and was transformed.

Later,
when you face old age and its natural conclusion
your courage will still be shown in the little ways,
each spring will be a sword you'll sharpen,
those you love will live in a fever of love,
and you'll bargain with the calendar
and at the last moment
when death opens the back door
you'll put on your carpet slippers
and stride out.

Anne Sexton (1928-1974)

The Narrow Way

Believe not those who say
   The upward path is smooth,
Lest thou shouldst stumble in the way,
   And faint before the truth.

It is the only road
   Unto the realms of joy;
But he who seeks that blest abode
   Must all his powers employ.

Bright hopes and pure delights
   Upon his course may beam,
And there, amid the sternest heights
   The sweetest flowerets gleam.

On all her breezes borne,
   Earth yields no scents like those;
But he that dares not grasp the thorn
   Should never crave the rose.

Arm – arm thee for the fight!
   Cast useless loads away;
Watch through the darkest hours of night,
   Toil through the hottest day.

Crush pride into the dust,
   Or thou must needs be slack;
And trample down rebellious lust,
   Or it will hold thee back.

Seek not thy honour here;
   Waive pleasure and renown;
The world's dread scoff undaunted bear,
   And face its deadliest frown.

To labour and to love,
   To pardon and endure,
To lift thy heart to God above,
   And keep thy conscience pure;

Be this thy constant aim,
   Thy hope, thy chief delight;
What matter who should whisper blame,
   Or who should scorn or slight?

What matter, if thy God approve,
   And if, within thy breast,
Thou feel the comfort of His love,
   The earnest of His rest?

Anne Brontë (1820-1849)

'throw
your soul
wide
open to
the light'

Progress
Ella Wheeler Wilcox

In this short Life that only lasts an hour

In this short Life that only lasts an hour
How much – how little – is within our power

Emily Dickinson (1830–1886)

The Common Road

I want to travel the common road
With the great crowd surging by,
Where there's many a laugh and many a load,
And many a smile and sigh.
I want to be on the common way
With its endless tramping feet,
In the summer bright and winter gray,
In the noonday sun and heat.
In the cool of evening with shadows nigh,
At dawn, when the sun breaks clear,
I want the great crowd passing by,
To ken what they see and hear.
I want to be one of the common herd,
Not live in a sheltered way,
Want to be thrilled, want to be stirred
By the great crowd day by day;
To glimpse the restful valleys deep,

To toil up the rugged hill,
To see the brooks which shyly creep,
To have the torrents thrill.
I want to laugh with the common man
Wherever he chance to be,
I want to aid him when I can
Whenever there's need of me.
I want to lend a helping hand
Over the rough and steep
To a child too young to understand –
To comfort those who weep.
I want to live and work and plan
With the great crowd surging by,
To mingle with the common man,
No better or worse than I.

Silas H Perkins (dates unknown)

I May, I Might, I Must

If you will tell me why the fen
appears impassable, I then
will tell you why I think that I
can get across it if I try.

Marianne Moore (1887-1972)

Traditional Irish Blessing

May the road rise up to meet you.
May the wind be always at your back.
May the sun shine warm upon your face;
the rains fall soft upon your fields.
And until we meet again,

May God hold you in the palm of His hand.
May the road rise up to meet you
May the wind be always at your back
May the warm rays of sun fall upon your home
And may the hand of a friend always be near.

May green be the grass you walk on,
May blue be the skies above you,
May pure be the joys that surround you,
May true be the hearts that love you.

Anon

The Good Joan

Along the thousand roads of France,
Now there, now here, swift as a glance,
A cloud, a mist blown down the sky,
Good Joan of Arc goes riding by.

In Domremy at candlelight,
The orchards blowing rose and white
About the shadowy houses lie;
And Joan of Arc goes riding by.

On Avignon there falls a hush,
Brief as the singing of a thrush
Across old gardens April-high;
And Joan of Arc goes riding by.

The women bring the apples in,
Round Arles when the long gusts begin,
Then sit them down to sob and cry;
And Joan of Arc goes riding by.

Dim fall the hoofs down old Calais;
In Tours a flash of silver-gray,
Like flaw of rain in a clear sky;
And Joan of Arc goes riding by.

Who saith that ancient France shall fail,
A rotting leaf driv'n down the gale?
Then her sons know not how to die;
Then good God dwells no more on high!

Tours, Arles, and Domremy reply!
For Joan of Arc goes riding by.

Lizette Woodworth Reese (1856–1935)

Character of the Happy Warrior
Extract

Who is the happy Warrior? Who is he
That every man in arms should wish to be?
– It is the generous Spirit, who, when brought
Among the tasks of real life, hath wrought
Upon the plan that pleased his boyish thought:
Whose high endeavours are an inward light
That makes the path before him always bright;
Who, with a natural instinct to discern
What knowledge can perform, is diligent to learn,
Abides by this resolve, and stops not there,
But makes his moral being his prime care;
Who, doomed to go in company with Pain,
And Fear, and Bloodshed, miserable train!
Turns his necessity to glorious gain;
In face of these doth exercise a power
Which is our human nature's highest dower:
Controls them and subdues, transmutes, bereaves
Of their bad influence, and their good receives:
By objects, which might force the soul to abate
Her feeling, rendered more compassionate;
Is placable – because occasions rise
So often that demand such sacrifice;
More skilful in self-knowledge, even more pure,
As tempted more; more able to endure,
As more exposed to suffering and distress;

Thence, also, more alive to tenderness.
…
And, through the heat of conflict, keeps the law
In calmness made, and sees what he foresaw:
Or if an unexpected call succeed,
Come when it will, is equal to the need:
– He who, though thus endued as with a sense
And faculty for storm and turbulence,
Is yet a Soul whose master-bias leans
To homefelt pleasures and to gentle scenes;
Sweet images! which, wheresoe'er he be,
Are at his heart; and such fidelity
It is his darling passion to approve;
More brave for this, that he hath much to love: –
'Tis, finally, the Man, who, lifted high,
Conspicuous object in a Nation's eye,
Or left unthought-of in obscurity, –
Who, with a toward or untoward lot,
Prosperous or adverse, to his wish or not,
Plays, in the many games of life, that one
Where what he most doth value must be won:
Whom neither shape or danger can dismay,
Nor thought of tender happiness betray;
Who, not content that former worth stand fast,
Looks forward, persevering to the last,

From well to better, daily self-surpast:
Who, whether praise of him must walk the earth
For ever, and to noble deeds give birth,
Or he must fall, to sleep without his fame,
And leave a dead unprofitable name,
Finds comfort in himself and in his cause;
And, while the mortal mist is gathering, draws
His breath in confidence of Heaven's applause:
This is the happy Warrior; this is he
That every man in arms should wish to be.

William Wordsworth (1770-1850)

'in the Sun, my wings can be display'd'

On Myselfe
Anne Finch, Countess of Winchilsea

I could not hide
From *Aurora Leigh*, Book I

I could not hide
My quickening inner life from those at watch.
They saw a light at a window now and then,
They had not set there. Who had set it there?
My father's sister started when she caught
My soul agaze in my eyes. She could not say
I had no business with a sort of soul,
But plainly she objected, – and demurred,
That souls were dangerous things to carry straight
Through all the spilt saltpetre of the world.

She said sometimes, 'Aurora, have you done
Your task this morning? – have you read that book?
And are you ready for the crochet here?' –
As if she said, 'I know there's something wrong;
I know I have not ground you down enough
To flatten and bake you to a wholesome crust
For household uses and proprieties,
Before the rain has got into my barn
And set the grains a-sprouting. What, you're green
With out-door impudence? you almost grow?'
To which I answered, 'Would she hear my task,
And verify my abstract of the book?
And should I sit down to the crochet work?
Was such her pleasure?' … Then I sate and teased
The patient needle till it spilt the thread,

Which oozed off from it in meandering lace
From hour to hour. I was not, therefore, sad;
My soul was singing at a work apart
Behind the wall of sense, as safe from harm
As sings the lark when sucked up out of sight,
In vortices of glory and blue air.

And so, through forced work and spontaneous work,
The inner life informed the outer life,
Reduced the irregular blood to settled rhythms,
Made cool the forehead with fresh-sprinkling dreams,
And, rounding to the spheric soul the thin
Pined body, struck a colour up the cheeks,
Though somewhat faint. I clenched my brows across
My blue eyes greatening in the looking-glass,
And said, 'We'll live, Aurora! we'll be strong.
The dogs are on us – but we will not die.'

Elizabeth Barrett Browning (1806-1861)

Desiderata

Go placidly amid the noise and haste,
and remember what peace there may be in silence.
As far as possible without surrender
be on good terms with all persons.
Speak your truth quietly and clearly;
and listen to others,
even the dull and the ignorant;
they too have their story.

Avoid loud and aggressive persons,
they are vexations to the spirit.
If you compare yourself with others,
you may become vain and bitter;
for always there will be greater and lesser persons
  than yourself.
Enjoy your achievements as well as your plans.

Keep interested in your own career, however humble;
it is a real possession in the changing fortunes of
  time.
Exercise caution in your business affairs;
for the world is full of trickery.
But let this not blind you to what virtue there is;
many persons strive for high ideals;
and everywhere life is full of heroism.

Be yourself.
Especially, do not feign affection.
Neither be cynical about love;
for in the face of all aridity and disenchantment
it is as perennial as the grass.

Take kindly the counsel of the years,
gracefully surrendering the things of youth.
Nurture strength of spirit to shield you in sudden
  misfortune.
But do not distress yourself with dark imaginings.
Many fears are born of fatigue and loneliness.
Beyond a wholesome discipline,
be gentle with yourself.

You are a child of the universe,
no less than the trees and the stars;
you have a right to be here.
And whether or not it is clear to you,
no doubt the universe is unfolding as it should.

Therefore be at peace with God,
whatever you conceive Him to be,
and whatever your labors and aspirations,
in the noisy confusion of life keep peace with your soul.

With all its sham, drudgery, and broken dreams,
it is still a beautiful world.
Be cheerful.
Strive to be happy.

Max Ehrmann (1872–1945)

In My Craft or Sullen Art

In my craft or sullen art
Exercised in the still night
When only the moon rages
And the lovers lie abed
With all their griefs in their arms
I labour by singing light
Not for ambition or bread
Or the strut and trade of charms
On the ivory stages
But for the common wages
Of their most secret heart.

Not for the proud man apart
From the raging moon I write
On these spindrift pages
Nor for the towering dead
With their nightingales and psalms
But for the lovers, their arms
Round the griefs of the ages,
Who pay no praise or wages
Nor heed my craft or art.

Dylan Thomas (1914-1953)

Market Day

Who'll walk the fields with us to town,
In an old coat and a faded gown?
We take our roots and country sweets
Where high walls shade the steep old streets,
And golden bells and silver chimes
Ring up and down the sleepy times.
The morning mountains smoke like fires;
The sun spreads out his shining wires;
The mower in the half-mown lezza
Sips his tea and takes his pleasure.
Along the lanes slow waggons amble.
The sad-eyed calves awake and gamble;
The foal that lay so sorrowful
Is playing in the grasses cool.
By slanting ways, in slanting sun,
Through startled lapwings now we run
Along the pale green hazel-path,
Through April's lingering aftermath
Of lady's smock and lady's slipper;
We stay to watch a nesting dipper.
The rabbits eye us while we pass,
Out of the sorrel-crimson grass;

The blackbird sings, without a fear,
Where honeysuckle horns blow clear –
Cool ivory stained with true vermilion,
And here, within a silk pavilion,
Small caterpillars lie at ease.
The endless shadows of the trees
Are painted purple and cobalt;
Grandiloquent, the rook-files halt,
Each one aware of you and me,
And full of conscious dignity.
Our shoes are golden as we pass
With pollen from the pansied grass.
Beneath an elder – set anew
With large clean plates to catch the dew –
On fine white cheese and bread we dine.
The clear brook-water tastes like wine.
If all folk lived with labour sweet
Of their own busy hands and feet,
Such marketing, it seems to me,
Would make an end of poverty.

Mary Webb (1881-1927)

Shining in the Distance

Already my gaze is upon the hill, the sunlit one.
The way to it, barely begun, lies ahead.
So we are grasped by what we have not grasped,
full of promise, shining in the distance.

It changes us, even if we do not reach it,
into something we barely sense, but are;
a movement beckons, answering our movement …
But we just feel the wind against us.

Rainer Maria Rilke (1875–1926)
Translated from the German by Joanna Macy (b. 1929)
and Anita Barrows (b. 1947)

'I will not cease from Mental Fight'

Jerusalem
William Blake

Index of Poets

Index of First Lines

Sources

"Still I Rise" and "Call Letters: Mrs. V. B." from AND STILL I RISE: A BOOK OF POEMS by Maya Angelou, copyright © 1978 by Caged Bird Legacy, LLC. Used by permission of Random House, an imprint and division of Penguin Random House LLC. All rights reserved. Reproduced with permission of the Licensor, Little Brown Book Group Limited, through PLSclear. "Call Letters: Mrs. V. B." from Maya Angelou: The Complete Poetry by Maya Angelou (2015). Reproduced with permission of the Licensor, Little Brown Book Group Limited, through PLSclear.

'Icarus' from *Selected Poems* (1946) by Ronald Bottrall, reproduced with the kind permission of Ingeborg Bottrall.

'Speech to the Young: Speech to the Progress-Toward (Among them Nora and Henry III)' from Speech to the Young (1991) by Gwendolyn Brooks. Reprinted By Consent of Brooks Permissions.

'Ithaka' from *C. P. Cavafy: Collected Poems* by C. P. Cavafy, trans. Edmund Keeley (1975), published by Princeton University Press.

THE POEMS OF EMILY DICKINSON: READING EDITION, edited by Ralph W. Franklin, Cambridge, Mass.: The Belknap Press of Harvard University Press, Copyright © 1998, 1999 by the President and Fellows of Harvard College. Copyright © 1951, 1955 by the President and Fellows of Harvard College. Copyright © renewed 1979, 1983 by the President and Fellows of Harvard College. Copyright © 1914, 1918, 1919, 1924, 1929, 1930, 1932, 1935, 1937, 1942 by Martha Dickinson Bianchi. Copyright © 1952, 1957,1958, 1963, 1965 by Mary L. Hampson. Used by permission. All rights reserved.

'93 Percent Stardust' by Nikita Gill, © Nikita Gill, reproduced with kind permission by David Higham Associates.

'Variation On A Theme by Rilke', Denise Levertov, *New Selected Poems* (Bloodaxe Books, 2003). Reproduced with permission of Bloodaxe Books. www.bloodaxebooks. com @bloodaxebooks (twitter/facebook) #bloodaxebooks. From *Breathing the Water: Poems.* Copyright © 1984, 1985, 1986, 1987 by Denise Levertov. Reprinted with the permission of The Permissions Company, LLC, on behalf of New Directions Publishing Corp., ndbooks.com.

'A Litany for Survival' from *The Collected Poems of Audre Lorde* © 1997 by Audre Lorde. Published by permission of Abner Stein. 'A Litany for Survival'. Copyright © 1978 by Audre Lorde, from THE COLLECTED POEMS OF AUDRE LORDE by Audre Lorde. Used by permission of W. W. Norton & Company, Inc.

'I May, I Might, I Must' from New Collected Poems of Marianne Moore (2021) by Marianne Moore. Reprinted by permission of Faber and Faber Ltd, Penguin Random House.

"Wild Geese" by Mary Oliver from *Wild Geese.* Reprinted by the permission of The Charlotte Sheedy Literary Agency as agent for the author. Copyright © 1986, 2003, 2006, 2017 by Mary Oliver with permission of Bill Reichblum; Penguin Random House, Grove Atlantic Publishers.

'Shining in the Distance' by Rainer Maria Rilke, from *A Year with Rilke* trans. & ed. Joanna Macy and Anita Barrows (1996), HarperCollins Publishers.

'Then I Saw What The Calling Was' by Muriel Rukeyser from *The Collected Poems of Muriel Rukeyser* (2005) ed. Janet E. Kaufman & Anne F. Herzog with Jan Heller Levi, University of Pittsburgh Press.

"Now I Become Myself". Copyright © 1974 by May Sarton, from COLLECTED POEMS 1930-1993 by May Sarton. Used by permission of W. W. Norton & Company, Inc. Reprinted by the permission of Russell & Volkening as agents for the author's estate. Copyright © 1993, 1988, 1984, 1980, 1974 by May Sarton, from Collected Poems, 1930-1993 (W. W. Norton). Originally published in The Land of Silence (Rinehart & Company).

'The Awful Rowing Toward God', Anne Sexton (1975). Reprinted by permission of SLL/Sterling Lord Literistic, Inc. Copyright by Linda Gray Sexton.

Batsford is committed to respecting the intellectual property rights of others. We have taken all reasonable efforts to ensure that the reproduction of all contents on these pages is done with the full consent of the copyright owners. If you are aware of unintentional omissions, please contact the company directly so that any necessary correction may be made for future editions.

*If you enjoyed this collection,
how about trying another in the series?*

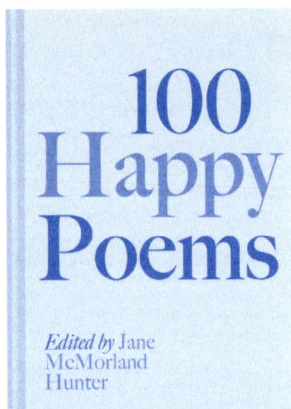

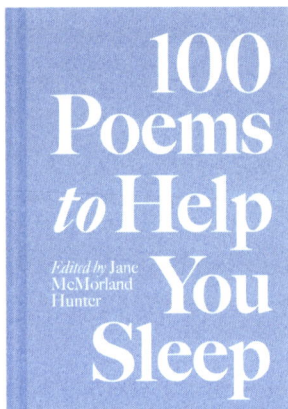

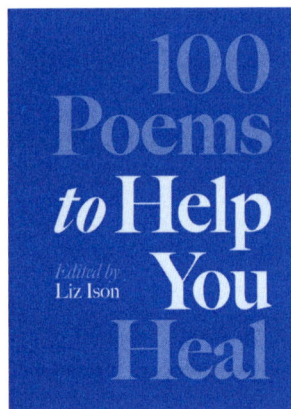

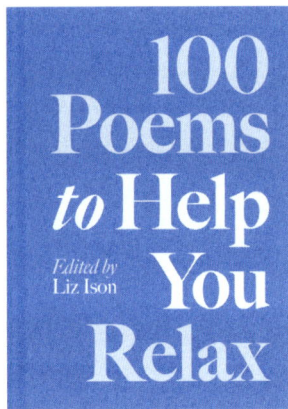

100
**Happy
Poems**

Edited by Jane
McMorland
Hunter

100
Poems
to **Help
You
Sleep**

Edited by Jane
McMorland
Hunter

100
Poems
to **Help
You
Heal**

Edited by
Liz Ison

100
Poems
to **Help
You
Relax**

Edited by
Liz Ison

These books can be ordered direct from the publisher at
www.batsfordbooks.com, or try your local bookshop.

Acknowledgements

A very big thank you to the great team at Batsford, particularly to my editors Magdalen Simões-Brown and Nicola Newman. Thank you, as ever, to The Reader charity for not only reigniting my own love of literature but also showing me, through the practice of shared reading and reading aloud, how to help people overcome the barriers that sometimes stand in the way of us enjoying and experiencing poetry. Thank you to my family and friends who continue to support and encourage my literary adventures.

About the Editor

Liz Ison studied English Literature at the University of Cambridge. Since 2015, Liz has been leading shared reading groups in person and online as well as workshops encouraging people to enjoy and rediscover poetry. Her poetry anthologies include *100 Poems to Help You Heal*, *100 Poems to Help You Relax*, and *A Poem to Read Aloud Every Day of the Year*. Liz lives in London.

First published in the United Kingdom
in 2025 by
Batsford
43 Great Ormond Street
London
WC1N 3HZ

An imprint of B. T. Batsford Holdings Limited

ISBN 978 1 83733 003 4

A CIP catalogue record for this book is available from the
British Library.

10 9 8 7 6 5 4 3 2 1

Reproduction by Rival Colour Ltd, UK
Printed and bound by Toppan Leefung Printing
International Ltd, China

This book can be ordered direct from the publisher at
www.batsfordbooks.com, or try your local bookshop

Distributed throughout the UK and Europe by Abrams &
Chronicle Books, 1 West Smithfield, London EC1A 9JU
and 57 rue Gaston Tessier, 75166 Paris, France

www.abramsandchronicle.co.uk
info@abramsandchronicle.co.uk

MIX
Paper | Supporting
responsible forestry
FSC
www.fsc.org   FSC® C104723